African Folk Tales

HUGH VERNON-JACKSON

Illustrated by Yuko Green

ISBN: 978-1-63923-873-6

Printed: March 2023

Published and Distributed By:
Lushena Books
607 Country Club Drive, Unit E
Bensenville, IL 60106
www.lushenabks.com

ISBN: 978-1-63923-873-6

Table of Contents

At the edge of the forest, the tortoise found some big eggs beside the river.

The Tortoise and the Leopard

ONCE UPON A TIME there was a tortoise who lived in a forest. She was a large, fat tortoise with a green and brown shell on her back, and over her stomach she wore a yellow shell.

One day she was going for a walk in the dark, shady forest where she lived. She came to the edge of the forest beside a river, and in the sand beside the river she found some big eggs. She recognized them as being the eggs of a crocodile.

Now the tortoise was very fond of eating good food, and she knew that crocodile eggs have a delicious flavour. She picked up the eggs and hurried with them to the compound of a family which lived near the river.

After the tortoise had greeted the family and the family had greeted the tortoise, she said, "Please, may I enter your compound, for I have something to tell you?"

"Certainly," replied the chief man of the compound, and he and his family allowed the tortoise to enter.

"If you let me use a cooking pot," said the tortoise, "and some firewood, some oil, and some pepper, and if you let me use three big stones to support the cooking pot over the fire, I will make a magic cake for you with the eggs which I am carrying. After you have eaten the magic cake you will always have good luck."

The chief of the compound and his family agreed to what the tortoise suggested. They brought a cooking pot, firewood, oil, pepper, and three big stones to support the cooking pot over the fire. The tortoise asked them to put everything in the room where the family stored its corn. When everything was made ready, the tortoise thanked the family, entered the room, and shut and bolted the door.

All day the tortoise cooked the crocodile eggs. She mixed them with the oil and the pepper and the corn which was stored in the room, and she made a very large cake.

When night came and the family were sleeping, the tortoise put the cake in a bag, left the compound very quietly and then ran quickly into the forest.

The next morning the people in the compound woke up. They looked for the tortoise but they could not find her. They knew they had been tricked.

Meanwhile, the tortoise was going deep into the forest carrying the bag with the cake inside it. The day became very dark, for there were many clouds in the sky. The tortoise heard thunder; then she felt rain. The day became darker and darker, the rain became heavier and heavier. The tortoise was beaten by the rain, but she did not dare return to the compound where she had cooked her cake, so she went on and on, hoping to find shelter. At last she came to the top of a little hill where, through the clearing in the trees, she could see smoke. The tortoise knew that the smoke came from a house and that where there was a house there was shelter. She walked and walked while the rain became stronger and stronger. At last she reached the house.

"Greetings, friend," the tortoise called at the doorway, "please will you let me in, for I am tired and wet from the rain?"

It was a leopard that came to the door.

"Greetings," said the leopard. "Come in."

Inside the house the tortoise found a warm place near the fire. She took her bag with the cake in it, and hung it up on a bamboo pole inside the house. As night had come by that time, the tortoise said good night to the leopard and went to sleep beside the fire.

The next morning when the tortoise woke up she saw that her bag was empty and that the cake had disappeared. It had been eaten by the leopard. The tortoise feared the leopard, so she did not say anything about the cake. Instead, she said, "I thank you, leopard, for giving me shelter. Now, if you will do what I say, I will make a magic powder for you. The magic powder will make you successful whenever you go out hunting."

The foolish leopard was very pleased and he agreed to do what the tortoise said.

The tortoise said that he should go out into the forest and bring forked sticks, four of them, each about six feet high. This the leopard did. The tortoise then said that the leopard should bring two strong poles to be tied to the tops of the forked sticks. The leopard went into the forest again and brought back the poles, tied them to the forked sticks, and drove one end of each forked stick firmly into the ground.

Then he allowed the tortoise to tie him to the poles and sticks.

"Greetings, friend, " the tortoise called, "please will you let me in from the rain?"

"When will you untie me?" asked the leopard.

"Never," replied the tortoise. "You ate my cake without asking my permission to eat it. Therefore I shall not untie you. I shall leave you to your fate."

The tortoise then ran off and disappeared in the thick forest.

After several hours some monkeys passed the leopard.

"Monkeys," said the leopard, "please untie me."

"Not us," replied the monkeys, "we are too frightened of you."

The monkeys went on their way. The leopard became very hungry. After several more hours an old mother monkey passed the leopard.

"Oh, Monkey," cried the leopard, "please untie me. I have been here for a long time."

The old mother monkey came back.

"Very well," she said to the leopard, "although I fear you, I will untie you."

The monkey freed the leopard, but she was not free from him. The leopard jumped on her and ate her up. After that, with a roar of rage, he ran into the forest to look for the tortoise.

The leopard went through the forest, but he could not find the tortoise. The leopard went beside the forest near the river, but still he could not find the tortoise. For ever afterwards the leopard searched beside the forest, and whenever one sees a leopard beside a forest, one knows he is looking for a tortoise.

The Story of a Farmer and Four Hyenas

ONCE UPON A TIME there was a farmer named Musa, who lived in a village five miles away from the nearest town. He was very pleased when his wife gave birth to a baby boy.

"It is the custom that you should have very good meals of meat for the next seven days," Musa said to his wife.

"With pepper," his wife replied.

"Pepper and meat I shall buy for you," said Musa, "when I go to the town."

On the following day Musa walked through the forest and the high grass of the bush to the town which was well known for its market. As Musa approached the market he could hear the drums beating which told him that the butchers had fresh meat for sale.

First of all, Musa bought a pocketful of red peppers. Next, he went to the butchers.

"Let me have four legs of a cow," Musa asked the butchers. "My wife has given birth to a baby boy and I must give her much meat that is sweet for her to eat."

"The legs make excellent soup," said the butchers as they gave the meat to Musa, "together with peppers."

Musa paid for the meat, and then spent the rest of the day visiting friends and relatives in the town. In each compound which he entered and to each friend whom he met in the street he said, "My wife has given birth to a boy."

Each friend and each relative replied, "I see that you have much meat to take back to her."

In the evening, after the priest outside the mosque had called for prayers, Musa left the town for his home. On his shoulders he carried the four legs of the cow.

Before he had travelled two miles it became dark. Now the part of the country through which Musa was walking was infested with very fierce hyenas. Soon Musa heard their laughing, and he began to walk quickly. Suddenly, in an open space beside the path, there was a rush of feet and movement on the sandy soil, and Musa was looking into the yellow eyes of a hyena. Musa at first stood still with fright, and then suddenly started to run as fast as he could go. The hyena came quickly after him, preparing to attack. In despair Musa threw down one of the cow-legs which he was carrying. While the hyena stopped to eat the meat, Musa ran on.

Before long, however, Musa heard another hyena laughing. He found another hyena in front of him, on the path. Again, Musa threw a cow-leg to the hyena, and while the hyena stopped to eat the meat, Musa ran on quickly, as quickly as he could go, and faster than he had run before.

But again another hyena appeared and threatened to attack. This hyena was larger and fiercer than the two others had been. Again, Musa threw a cow-leg to the hyena, and while the hyena stopped to eat the meat, Musa ran on as quickly as he could go.

Now Musa remembered that there was a small village not far from where he was and nearer than his own village. He turned and followed a narrow path which led to the nearer village, all the time running very fast.

But for the fourth time a hyena suddenly appeared. This hyena was even larger than the one before had been.

"I will eat you," growled the hyena and jumped towards Musa. Without hesitation Musa threw the last cow-leg to the hyena, knowing that there was nothing left to throw for hyenas to eat except himself.

He ran on and on until to his relief he saw in the distance the glimmering of a light which told him that he had nearly reached the village.

After looking into the yellow eyes of a hyena, Musa ran as fast as he could go.

As he was running towards the light, he found that all four hyenas were now chasing him. He tried to call for help, but he was so breathless that he had lost his voice. Just before the hyenas were near enough to catch him, he managed to reach the village and entered the first house he came to, where there were many people inside the entrance hall, sitting round a brightly burning fire. Musa fell on the floor, unable at first to talk, and breathing hard because he had been running so fast for so long.

The laughing of the hyenas outside the house told the villagers that Musa had been chased. The villagers seized their knives and axes and ran out to frighten the animals away. When they returned, they gave Musa some food and a place to sleep.

The next morning Musa thanked his protectors and returned to his own village. He told his wife what had happened and how he had lost the cow-legs.

"Only the pocket of peppers have I brought you," he said.

"Better that you lose everything," his good wife replied, "as long as you return safely yourself to your wife and child."

The next day Musa went back to the market in the town. He had only enough money left to buy one cow-leg. He told everyone his misfortune and his adventure, and there was no one who did not help him. The money he was given was enough to buy three more cow-legs.

The drums were beating and the butchers were again selling meat. Musa bought four cow-legs once more, thanking his good fortune. Not waiting for the night, but in the sunshine of the afternoon he hurried back to his village. On the way he thought he heard hyenas in the grass, but he was not sure; he thought he saw yellow eyes, but he was not sure. But he reached home safely. Thick soup was made for his wife. She grew strong. The baby boy grew well, and Musa and his family lived happily ever after.

The Greedy but Cunning Tortoise

ONCE UPON A TIME there lived on a hill an old and selfish tortoise. He was also a cunning tortoise.

This old, selfish, and cunning tortoise had a wife who knew how to cook delicious food and how to make very good soup.

The tortoise and his wife had a large compound. In it they kept dogs, cats, goats, hens, and ducks. Some belonged to the tortoise, and some belonged to his wife.

Now as well as being old, selfish, and cunning, the tortoise was also greedy. One by one he killed and ate all his share of the dogs, cats, goats, hens, and ducks. His wife cooked this food for him but he gave her very little of it to eat, for he wanted to eat as much as he could by himself. The tortoise's wife did not mind. "It is the way of my husband's character," she thought, "and I am used to it."

After the tortoise had eaten his share, he said that he would like to start eating the dogs, cats, goats, hens, and ducks which belonged to his wife.

"No," said his wife. "I will not let you eat my animals." She would not listen to his begging. "Nor will I let you eat my hens and my ducks," she said.

The tortoise planned to deceive his wife and by trickery to obtain what he wanted. He pretended to be very ill.

"Go quickly and pray," the tortoise told his wife, "and ask how I can be cured."

As soon as his wife had gone into the woods to pray, the tortoise left the mat on which he had been lying, and by another path went to the place where he knew his wife would pray. He hid himself in a hole and waited for his wife to come. When she arrived, the tortoise heard her ask how she could cure her husband's illness.

"No one can help your husband," the tortoise replied from his hole, "but you yourself."

"No one can help your husband," the tortoise replied from his hole, speaking in a strange, deep voice, "but you yourself."

His wife prayed again, asking how she could help him.

"Unless you give your husband your fattest goats and fattest animals, and also your fattest hens and ducks," the tortoise answered, "your husband is sure to die."

The wife was very grateful for an answer to her prayer and she hurried off on her way home.

As soon as she had gone the tortoise crawled out of the hole and ran as fast as he could by a short path and reached his house before his wife returned. There he lay down again on his mat and pretended still to be sick.

When his wife came back, she told the tortoise what she would do to help him.

"It is good news," said the tortoise. "Now bring me your fattest goats and fattest animals, and also your fattest hens and ducks."

When the wife brought her fattest animals and birds, the tortoise took them off into the woods. He told his wife not to follow, and he walked slowly like a sick man until he was out of sight of his wife. Then he ran very fast.

When the tortoise reached a small farm which he had in the middle of the woods, he killed all the fat animals as well as the fat hens and fat ducks. He cut them into small pieces and put them into a large black pot which he kept at his farm. He built a fire between three large stones and then put the pot of meat on top.

As the meat was cooking the smell became very sweet. The tortoise thought, "I shall enjoy eating this meat very much."

The tortoise then went away from the fire to look for crickets in their holes, because he wanted to eat crickets together with all his meat. While he was looking for the crickets a large and ugly creature all covered with long hair crawled out of one of the cricket holes.

"I smell your food cooking," said the ugly creature. "Carry me to where your food is cooking, tortoise."

The tortoise refused.

"Greedy tortoise," the creature cried angrily and said some magic words. At once, the tortoise's mouth and nose began to close. "Unless you do what I say," said the creature, "your mouth and nose will never open again."

The tortoise led the creature to where his meat was cooking. His mouth and nose opened, but not until the creature had eaten all the meat, every piece of it, and the tortoise was left with nothing.

"Now take me to your house," the creature said.

The tortoise took the ugly, hairy creature back to his house, and all the people were frightened of it. It lay down in the tortoise's room and went to sleep. While the creature slept the tortoise and his wife set fire to the room and burnt it down.

When the fire had burnt itself out, the tortoise looked inside the room. There were blackened ruins. The creature was inside, well roasted and smelling like very good-tasting food.

"I shall eat the roasted creature," the greedy tortoise said.

His wife advised him not to, but he ignored her.

When he had finished eating the creature, the head of the tortoise began to grow larger and larger. If the walls of his burnt room had not crumbled, the tortoise would not have been able to get out because his head became larger than the little doorway.

The head of the tortoise began to grow larger and larger.

Now the cunning tortoise planned a way by which he could exchange his big head for a small one. He saw a ram on his way to the river to take a bath. At that time rams had very small heads. The tortoise followed the ram.

"I too shall have a bath in the river," said the tortoise to the ram.

"Very well," the ram replied.

In those days it was the custom for animals to take off their heads and leave them on the river-bank before entering the water. The ram and the tortoise took off their heads. While the ram was bathing the tortoise quietly climbed out of the river; he fitted the ram's small head to his neck and very quickly ran away.

When the tortoise reached home, he and his wife put their belongings in baskets and ran away from the hill on which they lived. They went to a faraway valley.

"We shall build our new house here," said the tortoise, and they did.

Meanwhile, the ram had finished his bath, but on leaving the river found that his head had been taken away. Angry as he was, he had to have a head, so he put on the big one which the tortoise had left.

The ram ran to where the tortoise had once lived.

"Where is that cunning tortoise?" the ram cried, but no one knew where the tortoise and his wife had gone.

Promising himself that one day he would find and punish the tortoise, the ram went away. But he never found the tortoise and he had to keep his big head. That is why the ram's head is big and the tortoise's head is small: it is an exchange of heads.

A She-goat and her Children

ONCE UPON A TIME a she-goat told her children that they would go out into the world to seek their fortune.

They set out and reached a cave when night came. When they entered the cave in order to find shelter for the night, they met a hyena inside.

"Welcome to you," said the hyena. "I will give you food and water."

The she-goat thanked the hyena.

"I will go to fetch water for you," said the hyena.

The she-goat thanked the hyena again, but said that she and her children had decided not to drink.

"I will grind corn for you," said the hyena. The she-goat thanked the hyena, but said she would grind it herself.

The she-goat started to grind corn on a stone and as she worked she sang a song.

"My teeth are blunt," she sang, "and my mouth is tired, because I have been eating elephant and lion today.

Hyena, I come to you.

What would you have me do to you?"

When the hyena heard this song, she ran out of the cave and into the bush. Then the she-goat said to her children, "If I had not played this trick, the hyena would have killed us."

After eating their meal, the she-goat and her children lay down on the floor of the cave and went to sleep.

The next morning they got up and travelled all day along the road until night came. Again they found a cave and entered it in order to shelter for the night. But inside the cave there was a lioness.

When the lioness saw the she-goat and her children, she roared; she roared because she thought she would kill the she-goat and her children.

Then the she-goat started to sing.

"My teeth are blunt," she sang, "and my mouth is tired, because I have been eating elephant and lion today.

Lioness, I come to you.

What would you have me do to you?"

The children of the she-goat also started to sing.

"To be able to fight," they sang,

"To fight is our great delight.

We made the hyena run from us yesterday."

When the lioness heard this, she ran out of the cave and into the bush. Then the she-goat and her children ate the food of the lioness.

"We should thank ourselves," said the she-goat, "for playing this trick. Otherwise the lioness would have killed us."

They lay down on the floor of the cave and went to sleep.

The next morning they got up and travelled all day along the road until night came, when they reached a certain town where all the women were wicked. They entered the compound of the oldest, most wicked woman in the town.

"Welcome," said the wicked old woman, "and spend the night in my house. I will give you food to eat and water to drink."

The she-goat and her children thanked the wicked old woman and entered her compound.

"Here is guinea corn and here is a grinding stone," said the wicked old woman. "You must grind the corn so that you will have food to eat."

Then the she-goat started to sing.

"My teeth are blunt," she sang, "and my mouth is tired, because I have been eating elephant and lion today.

Wicked old woman, I come to you.

What would you have me do to you?"

The children of the she-goat also started to sing.

"To be able to fight,

To fight is our great delight.

We made the lioness run from us yesterday."

When the wicked old woman heard this she went everywhere in the town saying that the she-goat and her children had eaten elephant and lion and had made the lioness run away. Then the wicked old woman and all the people heard the she-goat and her children sing another song:

"Run away, run away," they sang.

"It is men and wicked women,

We shall eat today."

The people of the town became very frightened. Then, seizing their belongings, they left the town and scattered. They left the town to the she-goat and her children.

The she-goat said to her children, "If we had not played this trick, the wicked old woman would have killed us; she would have eaten our meat and made our skins into mats for the floor of her compound."

Then the she-goat and her children went to live in the deserted town, and ate the food that was there. They made their homes there, because they had succeeded in their cleverness.

The Boy in the Drum

LONG AGO there was a man called Yusufu who had a wife named Lade. They had only one son and his name was Hanafi. Because he was their only son, Hanafi was very much loved by his father and mother. His parents, in fact, always gave him everything he wanted and allowed him to do anything he pleased.

As Hanafi grew older he became very fond of hunting. One evening he told his parents that he planned to go hunting that night.

"Please do not go tonight," his mother Lade said. "I feel that tonight is unlucky."

"It is very dangerous," said his father Yusufu. "You are our only son, and we do not want you to risk death in the forest at night."

Hanafi refused to pay any attention to what his father and mother said. Finally they allowed him to go.

Hanafi went into the forest with several friends. They took bows and arrows, knives and guns and also lamps. When the animals came to the light the hunters killed two deer and six hares, and Hanafi was given his share of the meat.

As the hunters started back to their village, there was thunder and lightning in the sky. There was a great wind, and then there was heavy rain.

Hanafi saw a tortoise sitting in its house.

"Please may I have shelter from the rain?" Hanafi asked the tortoise.

"You may indeed have shelter," the cunning tortoise replied. "Here is a big pot you may sit in."

It was dry in the pot, so he thanked the tortoise and crawled inside.

As soon as Hanafi had entered the pot the tortoise took a large piece of skin and covered the mouth of the pot with it. With the skin tied on top the tortoise made the pot into a drum.

The next day the tortoise went to the king of the village.

"Your Majesty," the tortoise begged as he knelt on the floor in front of where the king was sitting, "may we have a drumming competition?"

"A drumming competition is a good idea," said the king. "We shall see who in the village makes his drum sound the best."

Three days later everyone in the village assembled at the palace, and all the skilled drummers also came. With them they brought their drums.

As the tortoise beat the drum, Hanafi, the boy inside, began to sing.

Yusufu, the father of the boy in the tortoise's drum, was amongst the crowd which came to the palace. As the tortoise beat the drum, Hanafi, the boy inside, began to sing. Yusufu heard the voice; he heard the boy singing his own and his father's names.

After the drumming was over, the king praised the tortoise, saying that the sound of his drumming was better than anyone else's. Then Yusufu went to the tortoise.

"Come to my house, tortoise, chief of all drummers," he said, "and you will be given an excellent dinner."

The tortoise thanked Yusufu and followed him to his house at the edge of the village.

While much good food and drink was being given to the tortoise, Yusufu told his wife to boii water. After his meal the tortoise lay down on a mat and went to sleep.

"Quick!" whispered Yusufu to his wife, "we will make him into soup," and they put the tortoise in the boiling water.

"Quick!" cried Yusufu to his wife, "we must save our son Hanafi."

He cut the skin on the tortoise's drum and brought out his son in time to save his life.

Ever after, Hanafi was an obedient boy who lived happily because he followed the advice of his father and mother.

Adamu's Mountain

ONCE UPON A TIME there was a very large hyena who lived on a mountain. The hyena's dwelling-place was a cave in the mountain-side, and it was so big that a man could stand upright in it.

At the foot of the mountain was a village of farmers and their families. All the people of the village feared the large hyena, and it was their custom to bring many presents to the cave and to treat the hyena with great respect.

One day a man called Adamu came from another village. He asked the people why they took presents to the mountain, but they would not tell him.

"I shall go to see for myself," said Adamu.

Adamu went to the mountain. Climbing the mountain-side, he found the cave and entered it. He walked far inside. Suddenly he looked back and saw the very large hyena.

"Let me out!" cried Adamu, but there was no way out. The hyena stood between Adamu and the door of the cave.

"Why have you entered my house?" the hyena asked in an angry voice.

Adamu could make no reply. He was too frightened.

"You are my prisoner," said the hyena, and he put Adamu in the food store at the back of the cave.

"Later I shall eat you," said the hyena, locking the door.

Meanwhile, Adamu's family, who had been travelling with him, wondered where Adamu could be. But his brother had heard him planning to go up the mountain. After two days the brother went to the chief of the village.

Suddenly he looked back and saw the very large hyena.

"Let me go to the mountain and look for my brother," he asked the chief.

"We shall look for him," the chief replied, "but we must take a present."

The brother gave the chief one of Adamu's fat goats. The chief, the brother, and many people went up the mountain-side until they reached the cave. The chief took the goat to the cave, and calling in a loud voice begged the hyena to let Adamu come out. Suddenly, Adamu came out.

No one ever saw the hyena again. When the people went back to take presents, the cave had disappeared from the side of the mountain. Ever afterwards it was called "Adamu's Mountain."

The Man with Seven Dogs

THERE ONCE lived a man called Manma who was a hunter and also a magician.

Manma had seven dogs. Their names were Tabantagi, Guye, Tako, Tifi, Etsuegu, Tazata, and Eyeshisoko. The dogs were well trained and were useful for Manma's hunting. Manma also had seven large black earthenware pots which he kept in his room. The pots helped him in his magic; they helped protect him from his enemies.

As well as the seven dogs and the seven pots, Manma had a wife. Manma and his wife very much wanted to have a child, but to their sorrow they had no children. The only help which Manma could obtain from his magic pots was their advice to ask someone else what he should do, so Manma went to a friend of his who was also a magician, and asked for his advice.

"Unless you have a lion's skin spread in front of your wife," the friend said, "not only will your wife have no child but she will also die."

Manma wasted no time. Taking his gun, he went into the forest, where he soon found a small lion, a cub, which had been left unprotected. Manma blessed his good fortune in finding a lion so quickly. He shot the lion and took the skin to his wife's room. Manma spread the skin in front of his wife and it was not long before she bore a child.

"We have been lucky," Manma said to his wife. "The magic pots directed me to the right man for advice."

Manma went to his seven black pots and told them that they had been successful.

Meanwhile, the lioness in the forest had discovered that her cub was missing. She heard from some monkeys in a tree that Manma had shot it and taken its skin, and she became very angry. The lioness changed herself into a beautiful princess and dressed herself in rich clothes fit for a princess.

She then followed the footsteps of Manma which led her to Manma's village.

Manma went to a friend of his who was also a magician, and asked for his advice.

When the lioness came near the village she met an old woman selling baskets.

"I wish to buy a basket," the lioness said.

"Sixpence," said the old woman.

"I will give you fourpence," the lioness replied. The old woman agreed and the lioness bought the basket.

When she reached the village she went to the market-place where there were many people, and amongst them she saw Manma. Many people greeted the lioness, she having changed herself into the form of a beautiful princess. Many asked her to come and be a guest in their compounds.

"I shall stay," she replied, "in the compound of the man who can throw a stone into my basket."

Many people threw stones, but all missed. Manma was watching, and his companions urged him to try to throw a stone into the basket. Manma threw a stone, and in that first try it fell right into the middle of the basket.

"I shall be your guest," said the lioness who looked like a princess, and she followed him to his compound. The first thing which she saw in his house was the skin of her lion cub.

Manma's wife fed the lioness, and when night came and it was dark the lioness was given a room in which to sleep. In the middle of the night she got up in order to go and kill Manma, but Tabantagi, one of Manma's seven dogs, stopped her.

"We have been warned," Tabantagi said to the lioness, for the seven black pots had spoken to the seven dogs. "If you kill our master, we will eat you."

The lioness went back into her room. After she had waited for a long time, she got up again, in order to go and kill Manma. Guye, however, another of Manma's seven dogs, stopped her.

Many people greeted the lioness, who had changed herself into the form of a beautiful princess.

"If you kill our master we will eat you," Guye said to the lioness.

Again the lioness went back in to her room. Again, after waiting for a long time, she tried to go out to kill Manma. Again, one of the seven dogs stopped her. She tried seven times and seven times she was stopped by the dogs. By that time the night had passed and it was morning.

The lioness saw no way of killing Manma on that visit.

Remaining in the appearance of a princess, the lioness thanked Manma for having her in his house as a guest, and she told him that she would be going away.

"I will escort you out of the village," said Manma, and he took up a gun.

"Are you going to shoot me?" the lioness asked.

Manma put down the gun and took up his bow and arrows.

"Are you going to kill me?" the lioness asked.

Manma put down his bow and arrows and took up a whistle.

"Let us go," he said, and the lioness agreed that they should go.

After Manma had escorted her for over five miles through fields and high grasses, they reached a river. Manma and the lioness said good-bye to each other and Manma began to walk back to his village. After Manma had walked for some distance, he found a locust-bean tree growing beside the path. He managed to climb up the tree just before the lioness, who had changed herself from the shape of a princess into her true shape, sprang at him in order to kill him. She had been following him.

Manma blew very loudly on his whistle. Immediately Manma's seven dogs appeared from the bush grass, first Tabantagi, then Guye, then Tako, followed by Tifi, Etsuegu, Tazata, and Eyeshisoko.

Before the lioness was able to run away, the dogs jumped on her and killed her. The dogs kept the meat and Manma took the skin.

"My wife," said Manma when he reached his house, "we had one child for our one lion skin. Now here is another skin."

The Story of Muhammadu

IN OLDEN times there lived a man called Muhammadu, a wood-cutter. The bundles of wood which he collected he brought to the market-place in the town to sell. Unfortunately, where he lived there were not many trees or bushes, so that the work did not bring him much profit.

Muhammadu had no wife, but he worked very hard in order to save enough money to be able to afford one. He dug a hole in the ground in his compound, and in the hole he hid his money. He put in the hole all the money he earned from his wood-cutting, keeping out only what he needed to buy food.

When Muhammadu had collected by his hard work and saved enough money to afford a wife, he dug up his money and left his town. He left behind him the gates and the walls and went to a small village in the bush. In the village he met a girl who agreed to be his wife. Muhammadu therefore went to the father of the girl and the marriage was arranged.

Everyone in the village came to the marriage celebration. There was a great feast, at which Muhammadu's wife received many presents—cloth, basins, pots, and corn. Muhammadu himself bought much corn and many mats, and he bought donkeys to carry the loads.

When it was time for Muhammadu to return to his town, he loaded his donkeys with the cloth, the basins, the mats, the pots, the corn, and all the belongings of himself and his newly married wife. He said farewell to the people in the village and he and his wife set out on their journey.

When they reached the gates and walls of the town, Muhammadu said to his wife, "This is the town where I live, and here is where we shall settle and prosper. This gate is where we shall enter."

There were many camels and donkeys and people entering the gates. Many of the people were greatly surprised to see Muhammadu the wood-cutter arriving with a wife and with donkeys heavily laden with goods and foodstuffs.

Muhammadu met one of the most important councillors of the town, a man whose title was Galadima. Muhammadu made polite greetings to the Galadima, and then went on with his wife and his possessions to his compound.

During the night thieves entered Muhammadu's compound and bound Muhammadu and his wife with ropes. The thieves had sharp knives, and they said they would kill Muhammadu and his wife if they cried out. So saying, they took the donkeys and the corn, the cloth and everything that was in the compound. They did not leave one pot, they did not leave even a needle.

The thieves had sharp knives, and said they would kill Muhammadu and his wife if they cried out.

The next morning Muhammadu and his wife were able to free themselves from the ropes with which the thieves had tied them. When they went out into the street, they told their neighbours what had happened. They went to the great compound of the Galadima in order to tell him their sad story.

Entering the compound of the Galadima, Muhammadu and his wife heard angry voices disputing the division of donkeys, corn, cloth, pots, mats, and other goods. It was the Galadima quarrelling about his share with several men whom Muhammadu recognized as the thieves who had robbed him. Muhammadu cried out to all the people. Pointing to his belongings, he called for justice against the thieves and the Galadima, who was their master.

"They bound us; they threatened to kill us!" Muhammadu cried. "They stole all that I had, I who as a wood-cutter had worked hard and saved my money."

These happenings were quickly carried to the ears of the Emir, who was the king of the town and of all the surrounding country. The Emir took speedy action. He drove the Galadima from the town for ever, he drove away the Galadima's followers and all the people in the Galadima's great compound.

The Emir called Muhammadu the wood-cutter, and the turban of honour was wound around the head of Muhammadu.

The Emir said to Muhammadu, "Now you are the Galadima of my town. You are the Galadima in my council."

For Muhammadu from that day on there was increasing wealth and power.

A Hunter, when the World began

AVERY LONG time ago, in the beginning of the world, there lived a famous hunter. He had killed so many wild animals that he had been given the title, King of All Hunters.

The King of All Hunters had two sons. When one of the sons wished to marry a young girl in the town, the King of All Hunters decided to test the strength and cleverness of this son.

"All the wildest, most savage animals I have killed," he said to his son, "except one. Go out into the bush. If you are able to kill this one remaining savage creature you will have permission to marry the young girl."

The young man prepared to go into the bush to hunt the savage creature.

"Remember," his father warned him, "what you are going to hunt is the most fearful animal in the world: with many mouths; with fire-like eyes; with enormous strength."

The young man took some food, then took his gun and his knife, called for his three dogs, and went off into the bush. He walked all day, and in the evening caught a hare for his supper. He walked all the next day and the day after that.

At last he came to the hut of an old woman who lived alone. She was outside her hut by a stream, where she was washing cooking-pots. She called out to him.

"I cannot stop," the young man replied, "for my business is urgent."

The old woman called to him again that it was very important for him to speak with her. The young man turned and went to see what she wanted.

"Here is food," said the old woman.

It was good food and the young man enjoyed eating it.

"Here is a calabash," said the old woman, "please wash it. "

The young man went to the stream and started to wash the calabash. But as he washed it, it broke. Inside he found an egg, a round smooth stone, and a small broom of palm-raffia.

"You have broken the calabash and I am glad," said the old woman. "Take with you what you have found inside. In case of danger drop one at a time, first the egg, then the small broom, then the round smooth stone."

The young man thanked her and went on his way.

The next day the young man reached a dark forest. He entered the forest, and at once his dogs started to bark. To his surprise, the young man suddenly saw the fearful creature which he had set out to hunt. The creature had many mouths, and fire-like eyes, and enormous strength.

The young man aimed his gun and fired, but the fearful creature only looked at him and grew bigger and bigger. The young man made a sign to his dogs to attack the fearful creature, but having looked into the fire-like eyes, their own eyes were blinded. The young man took his knife and ran to attack the fearful creature. They fought all that day, all that night, and all the next day, but at last the young man was victorious and killed the fearful creature.

The young man was glad, for he was now certain to marry the young girl in his town, and also he had destroyed a more fearful creature than any other hunter had done. The young man put the fearful creature on his back and started on his homeward journey. He left the forest and was walking through some woods when it became dark. He lay down to sleep.

The next morning was bright and clear, but as the young man woke up he saw coming towards him another animal, far larger than the fearful creature he had killed, far fiercer, and with far more fiery eyes.

He dropped the egg, and at once, there was a wide lake behind him.

The young man jumped up and started to run, with the wild animal following him. He remembered what the old woman had given him, and he dropped the egg. At once, there was a wide lake behind him, the greatest lake in the world. The wild animal still followed him. He dropped the broom, and at once there was the largest forest in the world behind him. The wild animal still followed. But the young man was nearing his father's house. He dropped the round smooth stone, and at once there stood the highest mountain in the world. But the wild animal still followed.

At last the young man reached his father's house.

"Quick, quick!" he cried to his brother who had been left at home, "open the door for me!"

As the young man ran in and the door was closing after him, the wild animal reached out and seized what he could from the young man's back before the young man escaped. And that is how the young man lost his tail and why no man in the world after that ever had a tail.

Koba, the Hunter who stopped Hunting

THERE WAS once a man called Koba, a hunter. One day he left his house and went off to hunt in a place which was far away.

When Koba reached a certain locust-bean tree, he made his camp under it. Every day he went out hunting, and every night also, resting only for necessity, to eat and to sleep.

One day when he was out hunting he suddenly heard the mighty roar of a lion very close to him. Never had he heard such a roar before. Greatly alarmed, Koba turned and ran as fast as he could towards his camp. He was carrying a bow and some arrows. On the way his bow caught in the low branches of a tree. He pulled but could not release the bow, and he thought it was the lion who had caught it, but he was too frightened to turn his head to look.

"Please, King of Animals," cried Koba, "let go of my bow. I have not come out to hunt you. You are the king not only of animals but also of human beings who are your Majesty's subjects."

Koba never turned his head. He waited for an answer from the lion, but as it was branches of a tree holding his bow there was no answer.

"If you are angry with me because of other hunters," Koba continued, "I promise to tell them no longer to hunt you. If you are too angry to release my bow, keep it. Only let me go free to tell other hunters not to hunt lions."

Again there was no answer. Koba left his bow and ran on to his camp by the locust-bean tree. Quickly he packed his belongings, and then made the journey back to his house with all possible speed.

"My brothers!" Koba cried when he reached his house and found two of his friends, "I have a terrible story to tell you of my escape from a lion whose roar is greater than any thunder."

After he told them his story, the two friends said, "Lead us to the place where the lion caught your bow."

"See, " said Koba, "the lion must have given my bow to this tree."

Koba led the two friends all the way back to the place. When they arrived, they saw the bow in the low branches of a tree.

"See," said Koba, "the lion must have given my bow to this tree in order to return it to me. The lion is not only the king of animals, but he is also the king of trees."

The two friends said that it was the branches of the tree which had caught the bow, not a lion.

"No, no," Koba declared. "It was certainly a lion. He pulled the bow and I pulled the bow, but the lion being stronger than me forced me to leave the bow with him."

From that day onwards, for the rest of his life, Koba never dared go far into the forest or the bush from his home. However much his two friends might laugh, he feared that he would meet a lion, and that the lion would remember his promise to tell all other hunters never to hunt lions again. Koba himself never hunted again: he became a farmer.

A Rich Man and his Goat

IN A SMALL town in the north there once lived a rich but foolish man whose name was Abdullahi. This rich and foolish man owned many sheep, many cattle, and many goats, but unfortunately Abdullahi had no sons and no daughters.

One day Abdullahi met the judge of the town.

"Because you have neither sons nor daughters," the judge of the town said to Abdullahi, "all your sheep, your cattle, and your goats will be given to the chief of the town when you die."

"Why is that?" Abdullahi asked.

"In this town," the judge replied, "that is the law."

Now Abdullahi was very angry when he heard this, because he did not want all his sheep, his cattle, and his many goats to be given to the chief of the town.

"I will sell my animals in the market," Abdullahi told his friends, "and I shall enjoy the money while I can."

When three rascals in the town heard what Abdullahi planned to do, they decided to play a trick on him and at the same time gain some advantage for themselves. When they saw Abdullahi go out of the town they greeted him. After greetings they asked where he was going.

"I am going to get one of my fat goats," Abdullahi told them. "I shall bring it to market and I shall sell it."

"We will be seeing you on your way back," the three rascals said.

After Abdullahi had gone, the rascals separated, each going to a different place beside the path where they waited for two hours.

After two hours had passed the first rascal saw Abdullahi on his way back, carrying a fat goat on his shoulder. The first rascal greeted Abdullahi very politely and humbly; then he said, as if he were saying a shameful thing, "It disappoints me, my friend, to see a gentleman like you carrying a pig, which is against our religion, instead of a goat."

Abdullahi was very surprised. He put his hand to his head.

"You cannot think I am carrying a pig," he said, and he went on his way.

Abdullahi had not gone far when he saw the second rascal sitting by the side of the path. The rascal was pretending to finger his string of beads and to pray. Abdullahi stopped to ask the pious man for his blessing.

"How can I bless you," the rascal said, "when you are carrying a pig?"

Abdullahi had not gone far when he saw the second rascal pretending to finger his string of beads and to pray.

Abdullahi rubbed his eyes as if he were trying to see what was the truth. Without a word, but with a much troubled mind, he went on his way.

Abdullahi reached the third rascal, who also had a string of prayer beads in his hand. The rascal stood up when he saw Abdullahi and stepped to one side to show his disapproval.

"You are doing strange things," he said to Abdullahi, and he spoke with a stern voice. "You told me you were going to get a goat and now you are carrying a pig."

"Is it really a pig?" the foolish Abdullahi asked, and the rascal told him it was.

"When you reach the market," said the rascal, "all the townspeople will be horrified that you are carrying a pig."

This was too much for Abdullahi. He threw down his goat, thinking it was a pig, and ran into the town. He went to the compound of the chief of the town, and as he went he told the townspeople what had happened.

"I am not well," Abdullahi cried when he and the townspeople came before the chief. He told the chief the story of what had happened.

But the chief and the townspeople understood how the foolish Abdullahi had been tricked out of his goat and they laughed and laughed at Abdullahi's great foolishness.

Meanwhile, the three rascals had caught the goat which Abdullahi had thrown down. They took it to another market and sold it, and then divided the money among themselves.

The Story of Mullum the Soldier

LONG AGO there lived a man called Mullum. He was a great soldier, and he was the leader of all the soldiers in his country. He was respected in his own country and he was feared in all the neighbouring countries.

One day Mullum went out hunting on his war horse, a black animal, and, like his master, very strong and brave. The war horse was also a great jumper, and could leap over rocks and streams. Mullum naturally valued him very much.

Now on the day that Mullum went hunting he saw no animals at all. Because of that he went farther and farther away from his town, and deeper and deeper into the forest. He went so deep into the forest that unknown to him he left his own country and went into the country of his enemies.

As he had travelled a long way, Mullum grew tired. Dismounting from his horse, he put a piece of rope between the horse's front legs so that it could not go far away. Then he lay down in the shade of a tree with many leaves and went to sleep.

It happened that some of the enemies of Mullum were also out hunting in the forest on that same day. Suddenly they saw Mullum's horse which had wandered away from its master while searching for green grass to eat. Seeing a horse with no one beside it, the men tried to catch it, but even with its front feet tied close together, the horse was too savage and strong for them, and the men hurried back to their town.

"Come quickly to the forest!" they cried when they saw their brothers in the town. "There is a very mighty black horse which we want to catch."

They returned to the forest with many of the bravest men of their town. There was a great fight, but at last the large number of men were able to catch the horse, and they led it back to their town, where it was taken to the palace of the king.

"May your life be long," the men with the horse greeted their king. "See, we have captured a fine black horse."

"I see it," said the king, "and I am overjoyed. This is the horse of Mullum, my enemy. Without his best horse, Mullum will not be able to fight so well."

The king gave orders that the horse should be tied up in the palace courtyard and be given freshly cut grass.

Now all this time, Mullum had been asleep. When he woke up, he could not find his horse. He looked all around him and he called, but in vain. Then he saw a man who was collecting wood.

"Greetings to you," said Mullum to the man who was collecting wood. "Have you seen my horse?"

The man had seen the horse being caught, but he did not like to say so. All he said was that he thought the horse had been taken to the near-by town. Mullum then realized that he was in the country of his enemies.

"Run to the town," Mullum ordered the man, "and tell the king that I am determined to search for my horse."

The man who had been collecting wood ran to the town and delivered the message. When the king heard the news he and several of his followers rode out to meet Mullum, whom they met walking along a path in the forest, on his way to their town. Mullum and the king greeted each other.

"Have you seen my horse?" Mullum asked.

"Perhaps," the king replied.

"Is my horse in your town?" Mullum asked.

"It may be," said the king.

Mullum demanded that his horse be returned.

"Be patient," said the king.

Mullum said he would go to the town to look. The king agreed, and they returned to the town.

"Here is a house for you to rest in," the king said to Mullum, "and here is fire and water and food. Sleep, for night is coming. Tomorrow we shall talk about the horse."

Mullum was unwilling to wait, but he knew that only by some trick, cunning, or good fortune would he and his horse be freed. He went into the house and found it comfortable. He tasted the food and found it good. He finished it, and then he lay down on his mat and went to sleep.

As Mullum slept, he dreamt that he saw a beautiful girl standing near him. He woke up from the dream and found that morning had come, and that there really was a beautiful girl standing near him.

"Who are you?" he asked her.

"I am a princess," she replied. "The king of this town is my father."

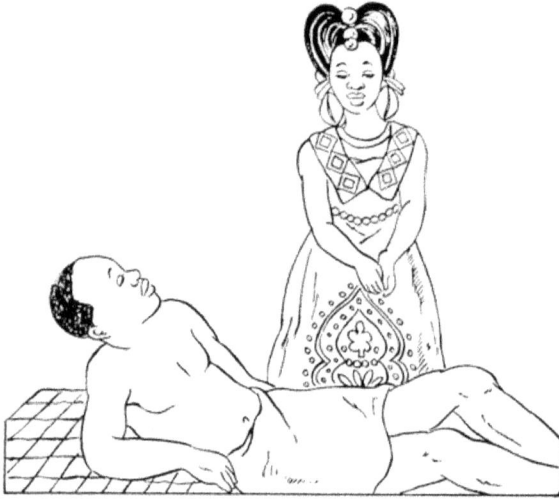

He woke up from the dream and found there really was a beautiful girl standing near him.

"Will you marry me?" Mullum asked her.

"Yes, if you ask my father's permission," said the princess, and she ran lightly away back to the king's palace.

Mullum went to see the king and asked for permission to marry the princess.

"I will give permission," said the king, "if you promise me that you will never fight against us again, and if war does arise between my country and the country of your king, you must let my daughter, the princess, return."

Mullum agreed to the king's conditions, and he also asked that his horse be given back to him.

"Take my daughter and take your horse," said the king. Mullum thanked the king. "Remember your promise to return my daughter if there is war," the king repeated.

Mullum left the town and went back through the forest to his own country, together with his horse and with the beautiful princess.

For half a year Mullum and the beautiful princess lived happily together. Then war began between the people of the princess's country and the people of Mullum's country. The father of the princess sent a message that she must be sent back to him without delay.

"I must go," said the princess to Mullum.

"Yes, it has been my promise," Mullum said. "Now there is war, so you must go back."

Preparations were made for the departure of the princess. Before she left, Mullum gave her a small square envelope made of leather which had been dyed red, and inside it was a magic charm.

"You will soon have a child," Mullum told the princess. "If you hang this leather envelope around the child's neck, there will be fame and fortune for the child during the child's life."

Mullum then said farewell to the princess, saying at the end, "If you give birth to a boy, I should like to know. Please send me a message."

The princess said she would do as she was asked. So saying, she started on her journey back through the forest to the town where her father was king.

The princess safely reached the town and the palace of her father the king, who welcomed her, and gave her a room of her own.

Not long afterwards the princess gave birth to a boy. Around his neck she hung the envelope of red leather which Mullum had given her so that there would be fame and fortune during his life. But the princess was deceitful, for she sent a message to Mullum saying that their child was a girl, and not a boy.

The child of the princess was given the name of Sahabi; he grew up to be strong and of good character.

"Tell me," he asked the princess, "who was my father?"

"He is still alive," the princess replied. "He is the chief of the soldiers in the next king's country and he is a famous fighter."

Sahabi himself was becoming well known as a fighter as he grew older, and he determined that he would go to the next king's country. He thought, "I shall conquer that country, and when I have done so, I shall make my father the king."

Sahabi made preparations for war, gathering soldiers about him. They went to the near-by kingdom, and after a battle they conquered that country. Sahabi captured that country's king.

"You are now my slave," said Sahabi to the captured king, "and I shall take you to show my father."

Before Sahabi could reach the town where his father lived, news reached the town that a strong young leader of soldiers from the country of their enemies had captured the king and was on his way to attack the town. It was Mullum who was chosen to lead the soldiers against the invaders. He had his famous black horse brought to him, and he called together his own soldiers.

The next day the two armies met. Mullum saw Sahabi and Sahabi saw Mullum, but they did not know that they were father and son. There was much fighting. The soldiers of one country fought the soldiers of the other country. Mullum and Sahabi fought each other. At the end of the day, all were weary, and each side withdrew to their camps for the night.

Mullum saw for the first time the envelope of red leather around Sahabi's neck.

On the following day the armies approached each other again. Sahabi called to Mullum.

"Leader of the enemy," he called. "What is your name?"

Mullum would not answer, for he was proud. He did not wish to speak with the enemy. When the fighting started once more, Sahabi, with his growing strength, knocked Mullum from his horse (which had become old and slow) and was about to kill him.

"Let me rise and fight again," Mullum cried. "It is not bravery to kill a man at the first blow."

Sahabi allowed Mullum to rise from the ground, and the fighting between them continued. Then Sahabi fell to the ground. Mullum drew his battle-axe and cut Sahabi across the chest.

"Alas," cried Sahabi. "All my attempts have failed. All my plans have been in vain. Now I am killed in battle in my search for my father Mullum."

At once Mullum realized that he had been fighting with his own son, and he saw for the first time around the neck of Sahabi the envelope of red leather which he had given to the princess for her child when she had gone back to her father.

Mullum sent a message to his own king asking for a special medicine that would help Sahabi, but the king refused, saying, "I will not try to save an enemy like Sahabi." When Sahabi died, his soldiers fled back into the forest from which they had come.

"Never shall I fight again," Mullum declared. "Through being a soldier I have lost my son."

And he lived as a peaceful man for the rest of his life.

A Good Fortune in Camels

A LI WAS a man who longed to go out into the world to see strange lands and seek his fortune.

He said to his wife, "Tomorrow I shall go out into the world."

She did not want him to go, but she was too wise to try to stop him.

The next morning, Ali set out on foot and walked until he found someone who would employ him for a short time. From that job he went to find another and then another, and so on until he had visited many strange lands. Of the money that he earned, he spent one-third on food and saved the other two-thirds. At last his thrift was rewarded and he was able to buy three camels with his savings.

As Ali was walking along with his three camels, he met another traveller.

"Greetings," said the traveller.

"Greetings to you," Ali answered.

They told each other where they came from and then the traveller said, "If you give me a present, I shall tell you something of value."

Ali gave the traveller one of the three camels.

"Do not go across any river which you do not know," said the traveller. "Wait until someone else goes first."

The man thanked the traveller, saying he was grateful for the advice. After going a short way, Ali met another traveller. They also greeted each other, and then the second traveller said, "If you give me a present, I shall tell you something of value."

Ali gave the traveller one of the two remaining camels.

"Do not rest," the traveller warned, "under a tree which has a big hole in it."

Ali thanked him, saying he was grateful for the advice. When Ali continued his journey, he met a young boy. After they had greeted each other the young boy said, "If you give me a present, I shall tell you something of value."

When Ali continued his journey, he met a young boy.

So Ali gave the young boy his last camel.

"Be patient," said the boy. "Do not show your first feelings of anger."

Ali thanked him, saying he was grateful for the advice. They parted and Ali, with no more camels, went on his way. He had not gone far before he met two camel drivers with thirty camels.

"Please help us with our camels," the camel drivers asked Ali, "so that each of us will have ten camels to lead."

Ali agreed and the three of them set off together with the camels. They came to a river which had flooded the fields on each side of its banks. The first camel driver took off his clothes and entered the water to look for the crossing. He fell into a deep part of the river and was not seen again. So the second camel driver and Ali did not cross there, but went on and found a safe crossing.

On the other side of the river they came to a forest. By that time the sun was setting and the men were tired. They looked for suitable trees to shelter them for the night. The camel driver took his sleeping mat and put it under a tree with a big hole in it. But Ali remembered the advice he had received and he moved away from that tree. In the middle of the night, a large snake came out of the hole in the tree and killed the sleeping camel driver.

When daybreak came, Ali saw what had happened. He was very sad and sorry for the two camel drivers. He set out and asked everyone he met if they knew where the camel drivers lived. He wanted to return the camels to their families. But no one could tell him and he lost patience. He controlled his anger, however. In time he realized that no one knew where the camel drivers had lived.

So Ali collected the thirty camels and went back to his own part of the country, to his home and to his wife. She was overjoyed to see him.

"You have not only seen much of the world," said his wife, "but you have returned safely."

"Yes," Ali replied, "and my good fortune in camels will bring us riches for the rest of our lives."

The Fisherman and the Ring

ALONG TIME ago there lived a young man whose father was a teacher.

"I wish to be a fisherman," said the young man to his father. The father protested, for he thought that his son would not make much money nor become well known. But when he saw that his son was determined, he reluctantly gave him his blessing.

Thereupon the young man bought nets and all the equipment that fishermen need. Then he built himself a hut by the river. At first he caught few fish, but with practice he became more successful and caught many more. The young man sold his fish in the market and gave the money to his father.

Then war came to that district.

"Help to defend our people," said the teacher to his son. So the young man left his fishing, took up his bow, his arrows and his spear and successfully fought the marauding enemies. By the time the fighting was over, there had been many losses in the village. But the young man survived and he returned to the river and became a fisherman again.

One day the son was in his canoe on the river when he saw a movement on the surface of the water. Quickly he threw his net and caught a fish that was bright red. To his surprise, the fish spoke to him, for no fish had ever spoken to him before.

"Do not kill me," begged the fish.

"All right," said the fisherman. "Just this once I will let you go."

"Thank you," said the fish. "For your kindness you deserve a reward."

"I should like money," said the fisherman, putting the fish back into the river.

The fish swam away, returning after a short time with a ring in his mouth.

"Take this ring," said the fish. "You can buy anything you want with what the ring gives you."

With trembling hands the fisherman took the red fish's ring. Excitedly he returned to the shore and rushed into his hut by the river bank. After closing the door, he turned the ring in his hand and said, "Please may I have money to buy a new boat?" Money appeared before him.

"May I have some to give to my father?" More money appeared before him. The fisherman ran back to his village and to his father. He became the richest man in that village and the last days of the old teacher's life were happy because his son had become so successful.

Then war came again to that district. The village was attacked. During the fighting the fisherman called to his ring, "Oh, ring, turn our village which they are attacking into the place of destruction for our enemies. Turn our attackers into stone."

Immediately the enemy were turned into a mountain which one can see behind the village. To this day the villagers speak of the fisherman, the talking fish and his magic ring.

The Magic Crocodile

THERE WAS once a very big cave. It was divided into two parts, the top part being dry and the bottom part filled with water. In the bottom part there lived a crocodile.

The crocodile did not live alone in the cave, for various other wild animals stayed there too. They lived in the dry part and various water creatures swam in the part which was filled with water. The crocodile spent most of his time in the water, but sometimes he would emerge from the cave for a short distance.

One day a hunter went near the cave in search of animals. He saw the crocodile resting in the sunshine outside the mouth of the cave. The hunter aimed his bow and arrow at the crocodile but immediately his eyes became blind.

When the hunter let the arrow fall from the bow his eyes opened again. He could see the crocodile smiling with pleasure at the cleverness of his trick.

The hunter did not stay, but ran back to his village and told the people what had happened.

"As I pointed my arrow at the crocodile," the hunter declared, "I became blind. The arrow fell out of my bow and then I could see again."

The people in the village grew very excited. Nearly half of them took up their bows and arrows and went off towards the cave.

"We shall catch that crocodile," they all shouted.

When the villagers came near the cave they saw the crocodile where the hunter had seen it, resting in the sunshine outside the cave. The very moment that each villager put an arrow in his bow and aimed at the crocodile, he became blind.

The villagers saw the crocodile resting in the sun outside the cave.

"Take your arrows from your bows," cried the hunter, and when they did so, the eyes of the villagers could see again.

"No man can harm me," said the crocodile, looking at the villagers. He got up from his resting-place and went back into the cave where all the animals praised him for guarding them so well.

"We will live our own lives in our village," declared the disappointed villagers as they returned to their homes. "That crocodile will remain in his cave. There is nothing we can do to change this."

However, some of the young men were not satisfied with this. From time to time, an exceptionally brave youth would return to the cave determined to kill the crocodile. But he never succeeded.

"Be blind with your bows and arrows," said the crocodile with a smile. Neither he nor the villagers had ever seen or heard of guns in those days long ago.

The Contest between Fire and Rain

ONCE UPON A TIME there was a king who had a beautiful daughter. Her beauty increased as she grew to the age of marriage and she was considered to be the most beautiful girl in the world.

Many men wanted to marry the king's daughter, but the first two to ask for her in marriage were Fire and Rain.

Rain went first to the king's daughter to ask if she would marry him, and she agreed; but Fire had gone first to the king to ask to be allowed to marry his daughter, and the king had agreed.

The king sent word that his daughter was to come to see him.

"I have promised to give you in marriage to Fire," the king told her when she came into his room.

"Your Majesty," the king's daughter replied, "but I have already promised to marry Rain."

"What shall we do?" cried the king and his daughter. "We are caught between two promises."

It was then that Rain arrived in order to visit the king's daughter; soon after that Fire arrived with the same intention. Rain and Fire were each determined to outwit the other.

Then the king said, "I have decided on the day of marriage for my daughter."

"To me?" asked Fire.

"To me?" asked Rain.

"To the winner of a race on the day of the marriage," said the king. "To him I will give my daughter."

There was great excitement amongst the people. Some said Fire would win; others said Rain would win. The king's daughter said to herself that whoever won the race, she would keep her promise to marry Rain.

When the day came for the race and for the marriage, it was very windy. The king made a sign and a drum was beaten. The race began. At first Fire was winning, for he was carried rapidly along by the wind. As for Rain, there was no sign of him in the sky. Fire continued to race faster and faster until it seemed to everyone that he would certainly win. When Fire had almost reached the place where the king sat with his daughter, Rain was at last seen preparing himself in the sky. It seemed to everyone, however, that he was too late. But when Fire was just about to win the race, Rain started to fall very heavily. Fire was quenched before he could reach the end of the race and Rain was declared the winner.

The king therefore gave his daughter to Rain to be his wife and there was much rejoicing.

Ever since that time when water quenched flames, there has been enmity between Rain and Fire.

The Hare and the Crownbird

ONE DAY the hare and his friend the crownbird went together on a journey. They were going to visit the house of the hare's uncle.

They travelled over hills and through valleys, until they came to a river. Beside the river there was an old woman washing herself.

"Please," the old woman asked the hare, "help me to wash my back."

"I will not," the hare replied.

Then the old woman saw the crownbird who was following the hare. "Please," the old woman asked the crownbird, "help me to wash my back."

"Yes, I will," the crownbird replied and began to help the old woman.

"Why do you bother yourself on such a task?" the hare said to the crownbird. "I will leave you to do this unrewarding job."

So saying, the hare continued on his journey.

After the crownbird had finished helping the old woman, she said to him, "Dip your wings and your legs into the water of this river."

The crownbird did so. Then the old woman told him to remove his wings and legs from the water. He did so. On his legs he discovered bracelets of great value and on the tips of his wings there were precious rings.

"Dip your beak into the water of this river," said the old woman.

The crownbird did so, and when the old woman told him to bring out his beak, he brought out beautiful clothing made of finely woven wool.

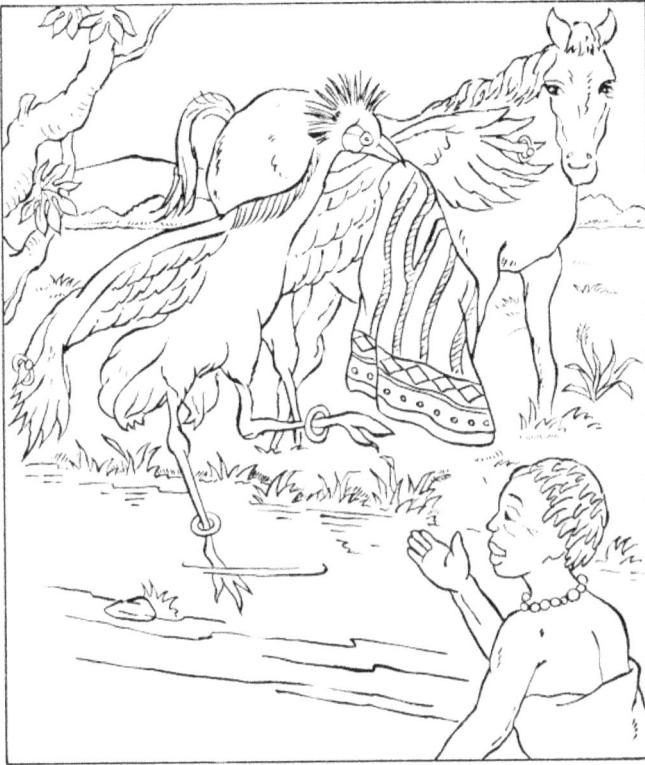

"The bracelets, the rings, the clothing, the horse—all are for you," said the old woman to the crownbird.

"Now once again," the old woman said. "Dip your wings into the water of this river."

Again the crownbird did as he was told, and bringing out his wings at the old woman's command, he found a very beautiful horse standing beside him.

"The bracelets, the rings, the clothing, the horse—all are for you," said the old woman to the crownbird. "I am grateful for the way you behaved when I asked you for help."

The happy crownbird mounted his new horse. It was a fast one and they soon caught up with the hare.

"How amazing," cried the hare. "You have bracelets, rings and fine clothes and you are riding a beautiful horse."

"Yes," replied the crownbird, "all this because of the old woman by the river."

Then he told the hare what had happened.

"Continue on your journey," the hare cried. "I'm going back to that old woman."

So he turned and ran off in the direction of the river.

When the hare reached the river, the old woman was still there. "Please let me help you," he said, smiling at her.

"Shall I take another bath?" the old woman asked angrily. "Shall I ask you again if you will help wash my back?"

"Yes, yes," cried the hare. "I will very willingly help you."

At first the old woman refused to be helped, but then because the hare continued to beg her to let him help she agreed. When the hare had finished helping her, she told him to put his legs and paws in the water of the river. The hare did so. When he withdrew them, they were covered with old and dirty bracelets and broken rings.

"Try again," said the old woman. But when the hare again withdrew his paws from the water of the river he held old and dirty clothing.

"Try again," repeated the old woman. But when for the third time the hare withdrew his paws from the water, he brought out the worst of all, a horse which was very ugly, short and thin.

The hare, with his dirty old bracelets, rings and clothing, mounted on his worthless horse and continued on his journey. The horse moved very slowly. Goats move better than that horse. Night had fallen by the time the hare reached his friend the crownbird at the house of the hare's uncle.

"I have learnt my lesson," the hare admitted. "It is better to give help than to refuse."

The Medicine for Getting a Son

AMAN NAMED Obi and his wife Ngozi regretted that they had no child, for they had been married for many years. Finally, Obi went to a wizard to ask for his advice.

"Go," said the wizard, "and bring me the milk of a buffalo, the tears of an elephant, the tooth of a lion, the tail of a monkey and the brains of a lion."

Obi left his wife at home and started out in search of all these things the wizard had named. On his way he met a rabbit. He told the rabbit that he needed the milk of a buffalo.

"I will help you," said the rabbit, and went without delay to a buffalo he knew.

"Honoured buffalo," said the rabbit, "see if you can run like me through the thick bushes which you see there."

The rabbit ran up and down making a lot of dust, and jumped right over the thick bushes, but the buffalo did not realise this. He crashed into the thick bushes where his horns became stuck. Whatever he did he could not free himself. The rabbit waved to Obi, who came and milked the trapped buffalo.

Obi continued his journey. He had not been going long when he found an elephant weeping for the death of his son. Obi again asked the rabbit to help him. The rabbit readily agreed and ran up to the elephant saying, "Honoured elephant, the tears of a prince should not fall on the ground."

So saying, the rabbit held a bowl to the elephant's eyes and collected the tears. He carried the bowl to Obi.

Obi told the rabbit that he still needed the tooth of a lion and the tail of a monkey. The rabbit ran back to the elephant saying, "The lions and the monkeys are laughing because you are weeping."

The rabbit held a bowl to the elephant's eyes and collected the tears.

His words made the elephant very angry. He marched quickly up to a lion who lived nearby and attacked him, but he only succeeded in breaking one of the lion's teeth before the lion ran away. Then the elephant saw some monkeys and before they could run away too he had pulled off one of their tails with his powerful trunk. The rabbit, however, begged the elephant to give him the broken tooth and the tail. The elephant agreed and the rabbit returned to Obi.

"Here is a lion's tooth," said the rabbit, "and here is a monkey's tail. Now I must go about my own business."

Obi thanked the rabbit for his great help, and he and the rabbit parted. While Obi was wondering how he might obtain the brains of a lion, a donkey passed by. Obi decided to follow the donkey to ask his advice but before he could catch up with him a lion suddenly appeared. It was the same lion who had already lost part of his tooth. The lion was still angry and when he saw the donkey he fell on him. The lion was almost ready to kill the donkey when the frightened animal suddenly kicked with all his might and cracked open the lion's head. His brains were revealed and Obi quickly ran up and took them. "The rest of the lion is yours," he told the donkey.

Obi returned to the wizard.

"Here is the milk of a buffalo," he said to the wizard. "Here are the tears of an elephant. Here is the tooth of a lion and the tail of a monkey. Here finally are the brains of a lion."

"You have done very well," said the wizard. "Now your wife will have a child, and it will be a son."

The wizard mixed together what Obi had brought him, and together these ingredients formed a medicine which Obi gave to his wife Ngozi. Before the end of the year the childless wife had given birth to a son.

When the son grew to manhood he caught the rabbit and bought the donkey.

"You helped my father," said the son, "and now I shall help you."

Obi's son fed and protected the rabbit and the donkey for the rest of their lives.

www.ingramcontent.com/pod-product-compliance
Lightning Source LLC
Chambersburg PA
CBHW051504270326
41933CB00021BA/3464